1 0 OCT 1990
2 5 MAR 1992
7 OCT 1993

- 4 NOV 1993

JS 796.334   RILEY, J.

                    Soccer

OXFORDSHIRE COUNTY LIBRARIES
SCHOOLS LIBRARY SERVICE

Resource
plus

OXFORDSHIRE COUNTY COUNCIL
LEISURE & ARTS

Schools Library Service
Tel: (0865) 810217

SOCCER

John Riley

Wayland

WORLD OF SPORT

Field athletics
Fishing
Gymnastics
Judo
Swimming and diving
Tennis
Track athletics

OXFORDSHIRE COUNTY LIBRARIES   796-334

Editor: Nick Wallwork

First published in 1987 by
Wayland (Publishers) Ltd
61 Western Road, Hove
East Sussex BN3 1JD, England

© Copyright 1987
Wayland (Publishers) Ltd

British Library Cataloguing
in Publication Data

Riley, John
   Soccer. — (World of Sport)
   1. Soccer — Juvenile literature
   I. Title   II. Series
   796.334   GV943.25
   ISBN 0–85078–967–2

Designed and typeset by
DP Press Ltd, Sevenoaks, Kent

Printed and bound in Italy
by Sagdos

Picture acknowledgements
Sporting Pictures (UK) Ltd 8, 9, 10, 11, 12, 13, 14, 21 (bottom), 22, 23, 24, 26, 27, 28, 29, 30, 31, 34, 35, 36, 37, 38, 39, 40, 41, 42, 44, 45, 46, 47 (top); *Mary Evans* 5, 6, 7, 8, 32, 43; *Wayland Picture Library* 15, 16, 17, 18, 19, 20, 21 (top). *Artwork by Ted Draper* 33. *Artwork by Andrew Popkiewicz* (RT Partners) 48, 49, 50, 51, 52, 53, 55, 56, 57, 59, 60.
The publishers would like to thank Andy Goram for his kind help and cooperation.

Contents

History of the game	4
Recent developments	9
A day with a professional footballer	15
Varieties in the sport	21
Players and teams around the world	25
Soccer grounds and stadiums	31
Championships and tournaments	38
Clothing and equipment	43
Fitness	48
Skills and tactics	52
Remarkable feats	61
Glossary	63
Books to read	63
Useful addresses	63
Index	64

History of the game

Ancient beginnings

No one knows exactly when football was first played. We do know that the game was played in China and Japan around the first century AD because at that time a writer named Li-Yu wrote what was probably the first-ever 'football report'. In it he describes 'a round ball and a square goal . . . and the two teams stand opposed'. It is not clear what the rules were, but it seems that the game had some kind of organization.

The ancient Greeks and Romans played 'throw and kick'. Again, the rules are doubtful but pictures show that it must have been something like football.

The game in Britain

It was not until centuries later that football was first played regularly in Britain, although ancient historians have found pictures of Vikings kicking the skulls of defeated enemies around the streets.

Soccer has come a long way since the early days of street football.

This picture shows some men in the sixteenth century enjoying a game of soccer.

The first regular reports of the playing of football in Britain started to appear around the eleventh and twelfth centuries AD. Unfortunately, the game made the news only for reasons of violence and often death. It was once described as 'more of a fight than a game', and on another occasion as 'more common, undignified and worthless than any other kind of game, rarely ending but with some loss, accident or disadvantages to the players themselves.' However, football became so popular over the years that the problems it caused reached the ears of the King on several occasions. In 1314, Edward II issued a proclamation complaining of 'great uproar in the City through certain tumults arising from great footballs in the fields of the public, from which many evils may arise.' By the end of the same century, football was still causing headaches and Richard II had it banned for a time, on the grounds that he felt it was preventing people from practising archery.

Many of the games of those days were connected with the religious festival of Shrove Tuesday. Reasons for this are not certain, but it is likely that it was the last chance for people to let their hair down before giving up the things they enjoyed for Lent.

For centuries informal games of football were played in Britain causing chaos as the players rampaged through the streets.

One venue for Shrove Tuesday football was the English town of Ashbourne. The two teams came from the north and south of the town and the aim of the game was to force the ball into either of the goals which were three miles apart. It all started in the narrow streets of the town and eventually spilled over into the surrounding countryside where much of the action, by this time a brawl, took place in a stream which ran close to the town. Over the years this game caused so much trouble and injury that the authorities tried all they could to bring it to an end. However, its popularity has survived into the twentieth century.

Organizing the game

Surprisingly, football managed to rage on in this undisciplined way until the public schools decided that it was time to civilize it and bring about some organization. Unfortunately it was difficult to do this because each school played to its own set of rules, but from this time on, football began to take on the shape of the game as we know it today.

The first football clubs

In 1862 the first football league club, Notts County, was formed and was soon followed by a number of others. Just one year later the Football Association was founded at an inn in London and was the first real attempt to organize the game nationwide. Shortly afterwards in 1873 the Scottish Football Association was also formed.

The game was now making great strides and in 1888, the Football League was founded. People may wonder why it was called THE Football League and not the English Football League – the answer is that it was the only body of its kind in the world at that time. The twelve clubs that formed the first Football League were Accrington, Aston Villa, Blackburn Rovers, Bolton Wanderers, Burnley, Derby County, Everton, Notts County, Preston North End, Stoke City, West Bromwich Albion and Wolverhampton Wanderers. How many of these teams are in the first division today?

The world game

All this time, football was gradually being introduced to the rest of the world. The British Empire was at its peak in the period 1875–1925 and it is probable that sailors abroad played the game in their free time and aroused the interest of the locals. So the first 'international' games were played between the local inhabitants and British servicemen.

Large crowds turned out to see the early Football League games. This picture shows Derby County in action against Notts County.

Naturally, just as in Britain, other countries wanted to play the game in an organized way and in 1904, FIFA was formed. The initials stand for the Federation of International Football Associations.

The game of soccer was spread throughout the world by British servicemen playing the game abroad.

International Matches

The first international match involving England and a foreign country took place when England toured Europe in 1908. First, England beat Austria 6–1 in Vienna then two days later they beat them again by an 11–1 margin! Hungary were then beaten 7–0 and Bohemia (now Czechoslovakia) were beaten 4–0.

However, the Hungarians had their revenge in 1953 at Wembley when they defeated England 6–3. This result ended England's historical supremacy in the eyes of the rest of the world.

Recent developments

A shrinking pool

It is sad to record, but football at all levels in the 1980s is being watched by record low crowds. Many reasons are given for this situation but most people believe it is due to the televising of football matches. At the same time, proof of the game's enormous popularity comes from the vast numbers who actually watch these televised games.

Many countries throughout the world televise games live and there is no doubt that football and television can work hand-in-hand for the benefit of the game, as in the USA.

Televised soccer is so popular today, that the commentators often become as famous as the players.

Women's football

Not long ago it would have been unthinkable for women to take part in anything as rough as football. Nevertheless, football is now played by a huge number of women throughout the world, and those who are amused by the idea should know how seriously the sport is taken by all concerned.

In parts of Europe, full-time professional teams play to packed crowds and attract players from all over the world.

Women's soccer is taken very seriously by many countries. This picture shows an international match between England and Belgium.

The USA, often thought of as the 'third world' of football, has possibly the largest number of women players anywhere and was one of only six countries taking part in the 1986 *Mundialito* – the women's World Cup.

Britain has tended to frown on women playing football, yet the sport has its own governing body, the Women's Football Association, and a staff of full-time officials.

Sponsorship

In the 1980s when attendances were falling and money was disappearing from the game at an alarming rate, a lifeline was found in the shape of sponsorship. Companies were allowed to put money into the game in return for the right to advertise their products on team shirts and on hoardings inside the grounds.

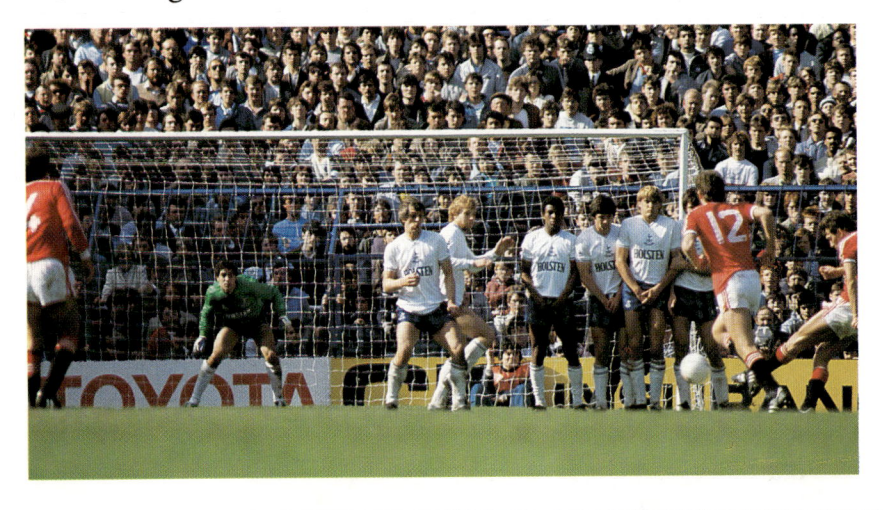

Every professional soccer team in Britain is now sponsored by a company.

Some clubs, such as Queen's Park Rangers, have laid artificial pitches to counteract cold and wet weather.

Money has poured into individual clubs in this way and companies have been quick to recognize the advantages of having their names linked to the major competitions as well. The Football, Scottish, and Irish Leagues, as well as the major cup competitions, have all borne sponsors' names.

Sponsorship has also spread to non-league and junior football and it seems that there are few competitions which are not taking advantage of what is on offer.

Artificial pitches

Football clubs in the southern hemisphere enjoy the kind of climate which makes play possible all year round in almost perfect conditions. European clubs sensibly have a mid-season break to miss the worst weather. Only Britain persists in trying to play without a break and more often than not, ends up with a pile of fixtures in April and May.

Attempts have been made to beat the weather conditions with undersoil heating. This has had mixed success, but too often clubs have been let down by the system at vital moments.

Two English clubs, Queens Park Rangers and Luton Town, went a stage further by having artificial, all-weather pitches installed. Such surfaces are common in places like the USA and have proved to be very successful. However, Queens Park Rangers met with a great deal of opposition at first and have had to make alterations to their surface. Luton Town on the other hand claim that theirs is as near to proper turf as it is possible to get.

These artificial surfaces have made a big difference to the clubs' finances:
- Games are not lost through bad weather.
- Training expenses are reduced as sessions can be held on the pitch.
- All games, including reserves and juniors can take place in the stadium.
- As there is no wear on the surface, facilities can be used at a profit practically twenty-four hours a day.

Tradition dies hard in Britain but it will be interesting to see how many clubs will move to all-weather pitches in the next few years.

Transfers

Throughout the history of the game, the size of transfer fees has caused sensations:
- The first transfer milestone was £1,000 when Alf Common moved from Sunderland to Middlesbrough in 1905.
- Denis Law became Britain's first £100,000 player when Manchester United bought him from Torino in 1962.
- Nottingham Forest became Britain's first million-pound spenders when they paid Birmingham City £1,180,000 for Trevor Francis in 1979.
- Napoli paid Barcelona a staggering £6,900,000 for Diego Maradona in 1984.

At the million pound mark in Britain, transfer madness took over and clubs were paying outrageous fees for moderate players. Many clubs paid fees which they could not afford. The whole scene became so chaotic that the Football League had to intervene. They ruled that in future, 50 per cent of all transfer fees had to be paid at the time of signing and the balance had to be paid within twelve months. As a result, transfer fees returned to more realistic figures, and clubs who could not afford to pay simply stayed out of the market.

Foreign players

For many years European clubs have lured star players from abroad in the quest for the game's highest prizes.

Italy were the pioneers of this trend but in recent years West Germany, France, Belgium, Holland, Switzerland,

Trevor Francis became Britain's first £1 million player when he moved to Nottingham Forest.

Tottenham Hotspur were one of the first British clubs to import foreign players. They shocked the world in 1979 when they bought the two Argentinian World Cup stars, Osvaldo Ardiles and Ricky Villa, to White Hart Lane.

Portugal, Spain and to a lesser extent the Scandinavian countries, followed suit.

Britain was about the last northern-hemisphere country to allow the import of foreign players, but since the decision was taken, some £10 million has been spent in bringing more than sixty foreign players into British football.

The emerging nations

Recent World Cup Finals have shown what advances have been made by previously 'unknown' footballing nations.

We have been excited by the skills of Morocco, South Korea and Cameroon, and impressed by the organization and work-rate of Canada, Australia and New Zealand.

In the 1970s and early 1980s many of the world's top players were attracted to the NASL.

The progress so obviously being made in these and a host of other emerging nations contrasts sharply with the failure of the outdoor professional game in the USA.

Many people are under the impression that football is a new game in the USA. In fact the USSF (United States Soccer Federation), the game's governing body there, held its seventieth Annual General Meeting in 1986.

The North American Soccer League folded in 1984 after seventeen years, during which time the world's best players were attracted to its teams including Pele, Cruyff and Best. The game flourished nationwide from New York to California, from Washington and Oregon to Florida. Proud names like the Cosmos, the Tornadoes and the Rowdies were blazed across the country, but now that is all gone.

In spite of all this speculation, the game is far from dead. There are hundreds of thousands of young players of both sexes learning and playing the game. The colleges have possibly the best-organized competitions of their kind in the world and scholarships are even offered in the sport at certain universities. More adults are playing the game than ever before, so it is not beyond belief that the USA could still make it to the World Cup Finals in the not-too-distant future.

A day with a professional footballer

Andy Goram is the goalkeeper for the English club Oldham Athletic. He is also Scotland's number two goalkeeper and was in the Scotland squad for the 1986 World Cup Finals in Mexico. This of course makes him one of the world's top goalkeepers.

We watch him in action on a normal Thursday practice day. Andy's training is typical of professional goalkeepers all over the world.

Andy lives in Oldham so it does not take him long to reach the ground. He parks the car outside the main stand where the changing rooms are and goes straight in to get changed.

He likes to be early as it gives him time to relax and have a chat with team-mates. They also discuss next Saturday's game at West Bromwich Albion.

The players soon gather on the training field. Today they are training on 'Wembley', the grass area at the back of the stadium, and not on the club's artificial surface. This is because next Saturday's opponents have a grass pitch and the Oldham coach feels that the first-team squad should have some practice on a similar surface.

Andy Goram is one of the world's top goalkeepers.

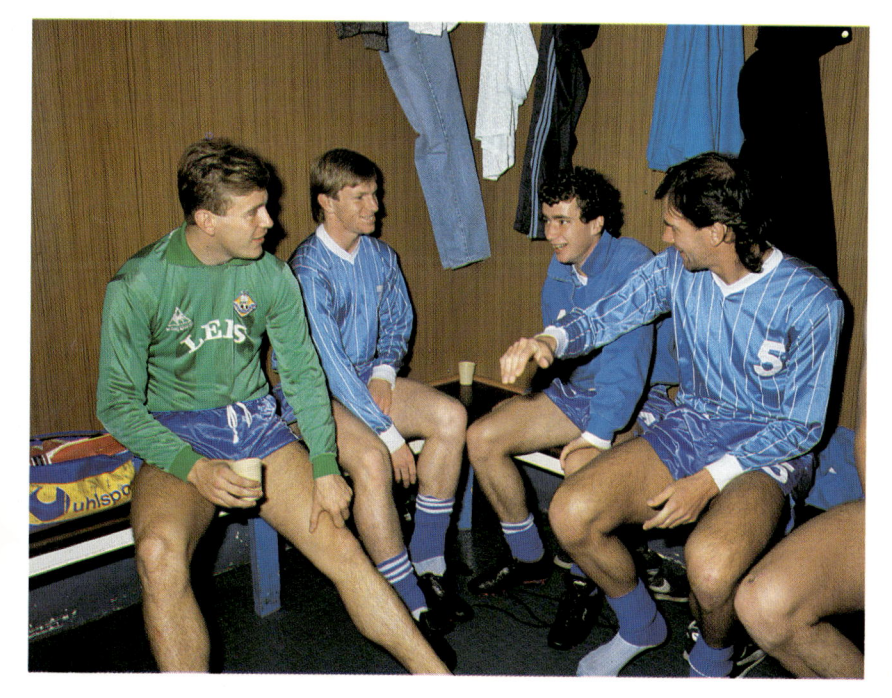

The Oldham players like to chat and discuss future matches while they change for training.

The players begin with a thorough warm-up with plenty of twisting and stretching. This is especially important for Andy as goalkeepers need great elasticity to perform the acrobatics required of them in a game.

As it is getting near to Saturday's game, the squad do not go through a session of heavy exercises. Instead they work on developing their skills, individually at first, with a ball each, then in groups where they go through a routine of familiar drills. Finally they work in larger groups, building up patterns of play which they use during league games.

It may not sound too strenuous, but half-an-hour of non-stop activity like this is tiring even for such fit players, and they are ready for a break before going on to the next part of the session.

The players spend a long time warming-up before the training session begins.

This phase is attack v defence and gives the squad's two goalkeepers (Andy Gorton is the other one) practice in a real match situation. The outfield players work on building up the kind of understanding which will help them to win league matches. The competition is keen as there are players who are trying to impress the watching manager and coach. Each play starts and finishes with the goalkeeper who sends the ball downfield for the attack to begin. Attacks start and finish with a strike at goal, so both goalkeepers are kept very busy. They take it in turns to keep the attackers at bay so they do have a rest occasionally.

Finally comes the 'fun' part of the session. The squad split

Andy is made to work hard in the 5-a-side game.

up into two teams – 'bibs' v 'track suits'. The game is played in a small area with mini-goals. There are no goalkeepers because the goalposts are very small. This is good practice for the two goalkeepers because they must use their feet to get in line with the ball and stop it with parts of their body other than their hands. So many players in such a small area places great emphasis on skill and everyone really enjoys the game.

Thursday afternoon is a very special time for the two goalkeepers. Every week at this time they have a coaching clinic with Alan Hodgkinson who was himself an England goalkeeper, so no one could be better qualified for this task.

Alan is a full-time goalkeeping coach and in addition to his work with English clubs he was recently appointed by the Scottish FA to work with their national squad of goalkeepers.

Competition between the two sides is keen as the young players try and impress the coaches.

Some of the players stay behind to help Andy with his training.

Some of the club's young players and one or two of the seniors stay behind to help with the session, which is divided into three parts:

- saving shots
- catching crosses
- goalkeeping in the game situation.

They are now working on the artificial surface in the stadium. First the outfield players take it in turns to keep up a barrage of shots. This is exhausting work as sometimes the goalkeepers are unable to hold a shot so they must also attempt to save the rebound. Fortunately they are allowed to work in turns.

The goalkeepers take it in turn to face a barrage of shots from the players.

Part of Andy's training session is spent catching crosses from the sidelines.

Next, the outfield players divide into groups and send over crosses from a variety of angles. After a while this is made even more difficult by using some of them to challenge the goalkeeper as the cross comes in.

Finally, the portable goals are brought close together and the goalkeepers take one each. The outfield players form teams of twos and threes to attack the goals so the goalkeepers are under constant pressure from a stream of shots and headers.

All through the practice, Alan has been calling advice and encouragement. Now, to end the session, he spends a long time with Andy going through all the points which he has noted to help him with his game.

At the end of the session Andy and his coach discuss any problems or worries that have arisen.

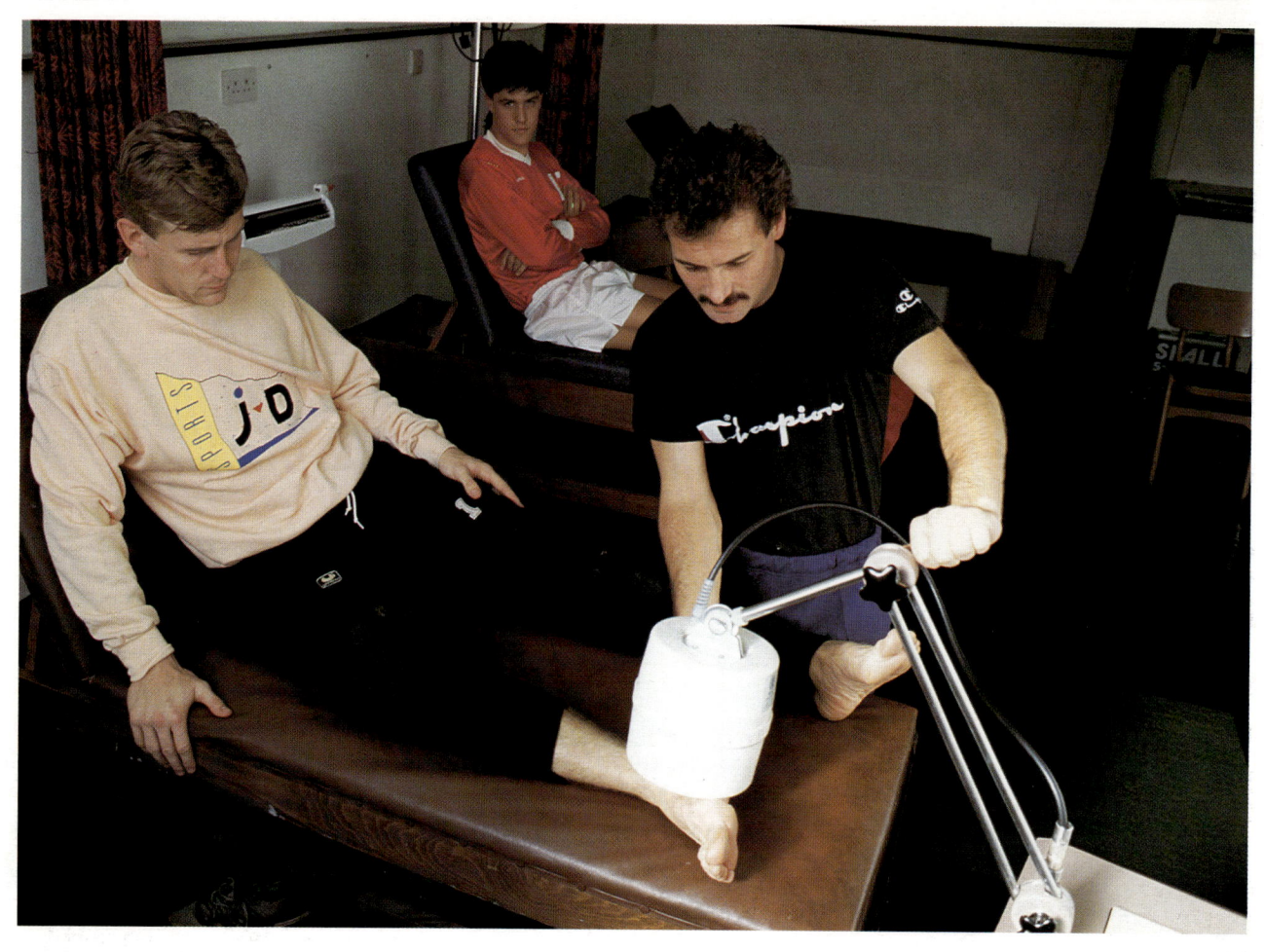

Any injuries, no matter how small, are always treated immediately by the club doctor or physiotherapist.

It has been a hard day and Andy, as well as being exhausted, has slightly strained an ankle, so a visit to the treatment room is necessary as a precaution. This gives us a glimpse of the frustrating and often sad side of being a professional footballer, especially for the long-term injured. They are forced to spend many hours on the road to recovery via the treatment table and progressive exercise.

Fortunately Andy's injury is not serious and the physiotherapist is able to put his mind at ease. He gives Andy some treatment to prevent swelling and the goalkeeper is able to go and have a welcome shower before going home.

It would be nice to spend the evening relaxing in front of the television, but Andy has recently started coaching a local team so he will spend the evening with them. Still, tomorrow should be an easy day so he will be able to catch up on some of the jobs which accumulate in a busy week before Saturday's vital game.

Varieties in the sport

Informal games

One of the beauties of football is that, although officially eleven-a-side, great fun can be had from knockabout games involving as few as two or three players. Almost every professional footballer must have learned his skills from playing street football.

Now it is hard to find a street which is not full of cars but that does not mean that informal games no longer exist.

All over the world young players can still be seen in twos and threes, juggling with a ball, shooting at goal, playing 'three and in', or attack against defence. If there are a few more players there is likely to be a small-sided game.

Small-sided games

It used to say in the Football Association coaching programme that small-sided games were the best way to learn to play the full game.

There is a great deal of truth in that statement. If we analyze a full eleven-a-side game it really breaks down into a series of small-sided contests – 1 against 1, 2 against 2, 3 against 3, and so on.

All the great soccer players learned their skills simply from playing around with a football.

Four v Four (3 v 3 + 2 goalkeepers)

Not only is the three against three outfield players game an ideal way in which to learn football, it is a practice much favoured by many top-class professional teams.

Four-a-side matches are used by all soccer clubs in their training sessions.

The advantages of three against three as far as young players are concerned are:

- There is plenty of room to learn the value of space.
- The small number of players ensures a great deal more ball-contact. This is far more enjoyable than standing around waiting for a pass.
- Three outfield players suggests a triangular formation which is the ideal basis for passing and positional skills.

With a little imagination one can see how a full-sized field can be divided into four small areas, with small goals, making four games of 4v4. This seems a far better use of players and space than eleven-a-side, where some players rarely see the ball.

Five-a-side

Formal five-a-side competitions are now a regular feature of the football scene from youngsters right up to professionals. The game actually evolved from the small-sided games used by most professional clubs in their training schedules. Rules vary regionally, but the following gives a general idea:

- Normal laws of the game apply throughout.
- If indoors, the ball may be played off the side or back walls and is always in play unless otherwise agreed.
- The ball must not be played above head height, and heading is not allowed.
- No bodily contact other than tackling but slide tackles are not allowed.

Five-a-side is a fast and exciting game requiring great skill and stamina.

- Only the goalkeeper is allowed in the goalkeeper's area.
- The goalkeeper must roll the ball out underarm and is not allowed to kick the ball deliberately.
- Some rules make restrictions on the ball being passed back to the goalkeeper.

FIFUSA

The initials stand for 'The Federation of Indoor Football in the USA'. This version of the small-sided game is also known as 'salon football'. A set of rules more rigid than five-a-side governs this game which began life in South America and is now played in Europe, Asia, Latin America, and the USA.

The game became so popular in the USA, that a body named USMF (United States Minisoccer Federation) was set up to organize it and it was renamed minisoccer. Minisoccer was seen as the ideal preparation for their professional indoor game.

The rules of minisoccer are different from five-a-side: there are five players on each side, a basketball-sized pitch, a special goal, and a small ball designed so that it has less bounce. Otherwise, the most important differences are:

- The game is controlled by four officials – a referee; two linesmen; and a scorer/timekeeper.
- The surface must be concrete, asphalt, astroturf, or wooden boards.

In FIFUSA a player is penalized by having to spend three minutes off the pitch in a 'sin bin'.

- The ball is out of play when it crosses the touch or goal lines.
- There is no height limit for kicking or passing the ball.
- Players other than the goalkeepers are allowed inside the goal area.
- A corner 'throw' is used instead of a corner kick.

The MISL (Major Indoor Soccer League)

The MISL is the USA's full-time professional answer to the rest of the world's opinion that soccer there is dead. Teams play in enormous indoor arenas holding up to 20,000 people and for the most part, the game has been a great success. Ed Tepper, co-founder of the league says of the game: 'Bringing soccer indoors provides all the right speed and scoring lacking in the outdoor game. They are the ingredients the American fans look for in a sport – and indoor soccer supplies them.'

The game's main features are:

- It is played on a green surface with a rocket-red ball.
- Teams average a shot on goal every minute.
- The game is six-a-side and free substitution of up to sixteen players on each side is allowed.
- Teams play four 15-minute quarters and if nothing is settled at that point, the first team to score in overtime wins the game.

The game hardly ever stops, with players using their head and feet and playing off the back and side boards, though players cannot just kick the ball to the far end of the pitch.

The American style of indoor soccer has caught on in Britain, and looks set to replace the traditional five-a-side game.

Players and teams around the world

One of the most enjoyable of pastimes when discussing players is to pick teams consisting of the best in the world. It is also a very controversial one as no two people will pick an identical group of players.

What we have done in this chapter is to make our own selections of players in an imaginary game:
International Stars against Former International Stars.
To make the task of selection more difficult, only one player has been chosen from each country on either team, including substitutes.

International stars

1. Peter Shilton (England)
2. Josimar (Brazil)
3. Antonio Cabrini (Italy)
4. Karl-Heinz Forster (W. Germany)
5. Alan Hansen (Scotland)
6. Vasili Rats (USSR)
7. Michel Platini (France)
8. Diego Maradona (Argentina)
9. Ian Rush (Wales)
10. Michael Laudrup (Denmark)
11. Emilio Butragueno (Spain)

Subs
(Goalkeeper) Ezaki Badau (Morocco)
(Defence) Cesar Zabala (Paraguay)
(Midfield) Liam Brady (Eire)
(Attack) Jan Ceulemans (Belgium)

Former International Stars

1. Dino Zoff (Italy)
2. Danny McGrain (Scotland)
3. Luc Millecamps (Belgium)
4. Franz Beckenbauer (W. Germany)
5. Mario Tresor (France)
6. Osvaldo Ardiles (Argentina)
7. Johan Cruyff (Holland)
8. Eusebio (Portugal)
9. Bobby Charlton (England)
10. Pele (Brazil)
11. George Best (N. Ireland)

Subs
(Goalkeeper) Dai Davies (Wales)
(Defence) Jose Pivarnik (Czechoslovakia)
(Midfield) Alan Simonsen (Denmark)
(Attack) Torbjorn Nilsson (Sweden)

You will no doubt have made your own choices by now. It would be interesting to get together with your friends and compare your selections. Whoever you choose for your teams, one thing is certain, it really would be fascinating to watch such a game. The pure skill and experience of the older players matched against the skill and fitness of the younger team would make a wonderful spectacle.

Teams around the world

Throughout football history certain teams have dominated the game then faded for a short time before returning as strong as ever. Others have faded never to return.

The teams highlighted in this section have been consistently successful for many years.

Liverpool

Few would argue with Liverpool's inclusion – they are perhaps the world's greatest team of recent years. One of the main reasons for their prolonged success is their policy of continuity as seen in their choice of managers.

This started in 1959 with the arrival of Bill Shankly. Since then Liverpool have gained an incredible twenty-four major domestic and European honours with a total of only four team managers:

Liverpool win the FA Cup – again! This remarkable team has been the most consistently successful side in the English league for the last fifteen years.

Bill Shankly   1959–75
Bob Paisley   1975–83
Joe Fagan   1983–85
Kenny Dalglish   1985–

Apart from Shankly they were all promoted to the manager's chair from within the club and all played for Liverpool. Each of these managers has shown an uncanny ability to find relatively unknown players, like Emlyn Hughes and Kevin Keegan, able to fit into the system and develop into world-class players. They have also been careful in their choice of foreign players like Craig Johnston, Bruce Grobelaar and Jan Molby who eventually became regular members of the team.

Celtic

Celtic have resisted the challenge of Rangers throughout their history, and more recently the threat of Aberdeen, Dundee United and Hearts. Their record in Scottish Football is awesome. They have won:

    The First Division   29 times
    The Premier Division   5 times (in 10 years)
    The Scottish Cup   27 times

In spite of this record, many felt that Celtic did not have the class to succeed at international level. Their reply was devastating. In 1966–67, one year after the appointment of Jock Stein, the club's former captain, as manager, they made

The Celtic against Rangers match often brings out the best in the two rival Scottish sides.

history by becoming the first British club to win the European Cup. They then added the Scottish League, Scottish Cup, and League Cup titles to this success.

Although Celtic's success has been limited to the home scene in recent years, the sight of their green and white hooped shirts is welcome on all Scottish grounds. Crowds are usually thin even in the Premier Division but Celtic's presence anywhere guarantees a large attendance.

Barcelona

Barcelona are reputed to be the wealthiest club in Spain today, but for many years they failed to satisfy the huge crowds who pack the Nou Camp stadium for every home game they play.

Barcelona's record in Europe is poor for a club of such standing. They have yet to win the European Cup, twice finishing runners-up, though they won the Cup Winners' Cup in 1979 and 1982.

Barcelona have spent enormous sums of money building up a successful side.

However, no one can fault their ambitions. At the start of 1984–85 they appointed Terry Venables as manager. He was an instant success, and in his first season at the club inspired the team to its first Spanish League Championship for eleven years.

There were fears that he might leave Barcelona, but he stayed to guide the club to the narrowest of defeats in the European Cup final of 1986.

Further proof of Barcelona's ambitions is their willingness to use their wealth to achieve success. In the past few years they have spent huge sums of money on top players such as:

Johan Cruyff £922,000
Diego Maradona £4,235,000
Gary Lineker £2,750,000
Mark Hughes £2,000,000

Juventus

Juventus are the undisputed kings of the Italian League, one of the toughest in football. They have won the league championship twenty-two times, almost twice as many as any other team.

Surprisingly their European record does not match their status, with only one final win in each of the three major competitions. However, success in the cauldron of Italian football is enough to satisfy one of the world's most fanatical followings.

Juventus have always had the ability to sign top-class foreign players who have blended well with the team besides retaining their own star qualities. Typical of such signings was the legendary 'King' John Charles who gave many years of outstanding service to Juventus.

In more recent years, European Footballer of the Year Michel Platini, and Zbigniew Boniek have thrilled supporters with their superb goals which are the most highly-prized currency in Italian football.

Another goal for Juventus: this one helped them win the European Cup in 1985.

Bayern Munich

Bayern Munich's achievements in West Germany are all the more remarkable as they were not elected to the *Bundesliga* (German National League) when it was first formed in 1963. They had to wait two years for promotion and two more years for their first league championship, although they were Cup-winners in 1966 and 1967 (when they also won the European Cup Winners' Cup). In all, they hold the record number of league and cup wins with eight and nine respectively.

Bayern Munich reached the height of their success in the 1970s with a hat-trick of victories in the European Cup in 1974–'75–'76. This team was inspired by the genius of Franz Beckenbauer and the goals of Gerd Muller but contained other international stars in Maier, Breitner,

Over the years Bayern Munich have provided the West German side with many of its star players.

Schwarzenbeck, Roth, Hoeness, and the young Karl-Heinz Rummenigge. The present team may be a little short of such class, but it is still the most powerful and consistent in the West German league.

Flamengo

The Brazilian club Flamengo, whose home ground is the 200,000 capacity Maracana Stadium in Rio de Janeiro, are probably the best-supported team in the world. Crowds regularly reach 100,000, especially for games with arch-rivals Fluminense. In 1963, 177,656 people turned up to watch this game. Flamengo have regularly won both the Brazilian state championship and the Rio 'Carioca' League, but surprisingly have won the South American Cup (Copa Libertadores) only once, in 1981.

In the same year they beat Liverpool 3–0 to become the World Club Champions and crushed opinions that Brazilian club football is a lightweight affair.

Flamengo's most famous players of recent years are Socrates – Brazil's former captain, and Artur Antunes Coimbra – Zico, the country's record goal-scorer and three-times South American Footballer of the Year.

Zico has provided many great soccer moments for his club and country.

Soccer grounds and stadiums

There is something very special about a football stadium. For a footballer or genuine supporter, there is nothing to compare with the atmosphere of a big game in which the stadium itself plays such a big part. So what are the individual components which together produce this marvellous atmosphere?

Stands and terraces

The most impressive features of a modern football stadium are the stands and terraces which tower over the pitch below. It seems that the bigger the club, the more imposing its stadium.

The stand in a way has become a club's status symbol. Wealthy clubs have increased the size of their stands to contain:
- Modern changing-rooms, treatment-rooms, and offices.
- Hospitality suites, bars and restaurants.
- Up-to-date press and conference facilities.
- Sports halls and gymnasiums.

The main purpose of a stand is of course to provide viewing facilities for spectators, and clubs are constantly improving these amenities.

(above & below) Security cameras and metal fences are just a couple of the measures taken to combat soccer hooliganism.

(left) Wolverhampton Wanderer's cantilevered stand provides adequate protection as well as an undisturbed view for its supporters.

31

Almost all big clubs have increased their seating capacity, sometimes to the extent of making their grounds all-seater. This reduces the overall capacity but it greatly improves spectator comfort and has the added benefit of reducing the effects of hooliganism.

The building of cantilevered stands has greatly improved the quality of viewing at most grounds. These stands have done away with the network of girders and other obstructions which used to support old-fashioned structures so supporters can now enjoy a clear view of the game.

Clubs all over the world are competing in the business of building bigger and better grounds. Unfortunately, events and trends over the years have meant that one aspect of this building has been forced on to clubs which is not welcome. Football grounds outside Britain have come to accept such things as safety-fences as a means of separating players from spectators. However, various acts of hooliganism in recent

Today's spectators enjoy a much better view of the game than those in this Aston Villa/Everton match in 1897.

years have forced the authorities in Britain to implement further crowd controls at grounds. The result, in theory, will be excellent as all grounds will be quickly brought into the 1980s. However, these compulsory changes will put many clubs under severe financial pressure, and what will happen to them in the future, only time will tell.

Wembley

Wembley is the most famous stadium in the world in which football is played. With a capacity of 100,000 it may not be the biggest, it may not have the most ultra-modern facilities in the world, but it has a unique atmosphere which makes it a favourite among players all over the world.

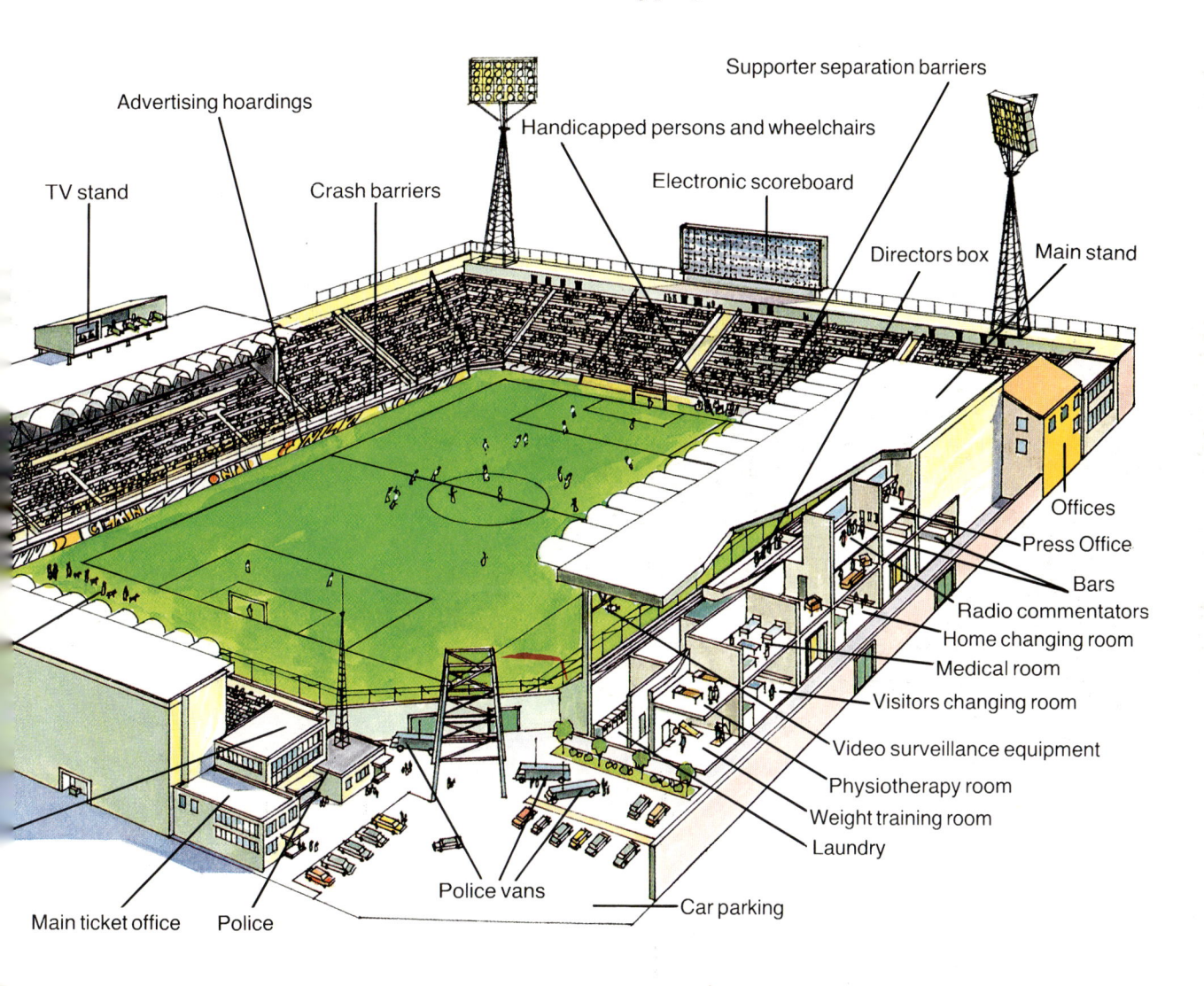

Wembley is probably the most famous soccer venue in the world. Its twin towers have overlooked many great games since its completion in 1923.

The building of Wembley Stadium was completed in 1923 in three hundred working days at a cost of £750,000. One stand alone would cost twice that amount today. Although Wembley hosts a number of other sports, it will always be seen as the home of English football.

The Royal Box, the stadium's most famous feature holds seventy guests. Television cameras are housed on the south side of the stadium and for any outside broadcasts, the equipment is hoisted into position by a lift.

The famous changing-rooms have recently been brought up to date with the latest designs in baths, showers, treatment facilities, and for each player, a personal numbered locker.

Old Trafford

Old Trafford, the home of Manchester United, is the most popular club ground in England – in the words of Bobby Charlton, 'a theatre of dreams'. The ground is the best-attended at club level in England.

Everywhere the stadium reflects the red glow of the club's colours and the fact that the ground is covered on all four sides produces a noise of unequalled volume.

The design of the stands is such that the cantilever roof is carried on right round the stadium. It is also intended that the number of private boxes (eighty at present and the first to be built on a club ground in England) will be increased.

The 'theatre of dreams' – these empty terraces at Old Trafford are packed with fanatical fans for every home game.

The record crowd at Old Trafford is 76,962 set up in 1939, but the present capacity is limited to 56,399 with 20,000 of these seated.

Ibrox

Ibrox is the home of Glasgow Rangers. Not many years ago, Ibrox was an old-fashioned stadium with mainly wooden buildings. It was so large that 118,567 spectators packed into it for the New Year game with Celtic in 1939.

However, the ground suffered three tragedies – in 1902, 1961, and 1971 – in which a total of ninety-four people died.

Due to three major tragedies the Ibrox stadium has had to be extensively rebuilt. The Archibald Leitch stand on the right is all that remains of the original stadium.

Since then £10,000,000 has been spent on modernization. The shape of the ground has been changed from oval to rectangular, the capacity has been cut to 45,000 (20,000 seated), and the ground is covered on all sides. Three sides are completely new and unrecognizable from the old stadium. The seats are an interesting patchwork of various colours and only the Archibald Leitch South Stand remains of the old stadium. Spaces between the stands have been landscaped, and there is a shale practice area under the stand close to where players and officials come out on to the field.

The Bernabeu Stadium

The Santiago Bernabeu Stadium in Madrid is the home of Real Madrid, Spain's most celebrated football team.

Real Madrid won the European Cup five successive times from 1956–1960 and at the time were unequalled in club football. They boasted a team of all nationalities which included Ferenc Puskas, Alfredo di Stefano, Francisco

The imposing Bernabeu Stadium in Madrid was built with money donated by the club's fans.

Gento, and Jose Santamaria, a team which would have been hard to beat even at international level.

The Bernabeu Stadium was opened in 1947 to provide Real Madrid with surroundings to match their world standing. Previously they played at a run-down ground in the area of the present stadium, but in 1946, Santiago Bernabeu, the club's former centre-forward appealed to supporters for a loan to help build new premises.

The result was astonishing. Money poured in and the club kept its word by building today's multi-sport stadium, the finest of its kind in Europe with a present capacity of 90,000.

The Maracana Stadium

The giant Maracana Stadium in Rio de Janeiro is the largest ground in the world on which football is played. It holds 200,000 spectators and has a staggering 165,000 seating capacity.

The stadium is part of a vast sports complex.

The Maracana Stadium is the largest soccer ground in the world, and has been filled to capacity on several occasions.

Championships and tournaments

The world football scene is a maze of competitions, with championships changing their names as new sponsors or more suitable titles are found.

What it all amounts to is an increase in the demands made on players at the top level. When a club is successful its players can be called on to play over seventy fiercely competitive games in a season which spreads over two-thirds of a year. Contrast that with American football, where even the most successful players only take part in around twenty games each season and you can appreciate how harsh these demands are.

What then are the world's most highly rated football competitions?

The World Cup

The World Cup stands alone as the most important footballing event of all. The idea was first thought of by Jules Rimet, a French lawyer, after whom the original trophy was named. The first World Cup was held in Uruguay in 1930 and was won by the host nation.

In 1986 Argentina won the World Cup for the second time, when they beat West Germany 3–2.

Forty years later in 1970, Brazil won the right to keep the Jules Rimet Trophy by being the victors in three tournaments. Italy have since joined them on that figure.

The World Cup finals have taken place every four years since that first occasion, except for 1942 and 1946 when the tournament was temporarily suspended. The venue is shared equally between Europe and South America, the two major football-playing continents.

The first World Cup finals had an entry of only thirteen teams. Now over one hundred take part in the qualifying stages and twenty-four reach the tournament finals.

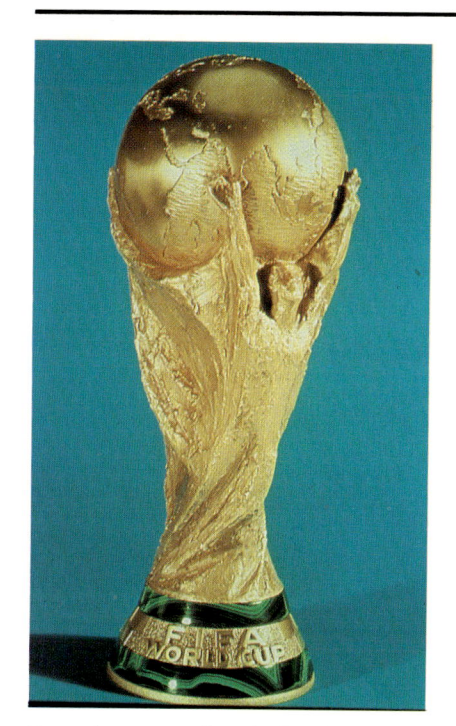

Every four years, twenty-four teams compete to try and win the most coveted trophy in football – the World Cup.

The European Championship

Close on the heels of the World Cup come the European Championship and the South American Championship.

The European Championship takes two years to complete with the final played exactly between World Cups. This competition was first held in 1958 as the Henri Delauney Cup after its founder. It later became known as the Nations Cup before being given its present title.

The honours have been evenly distributed over the years with only West Germany winning the title more than once, in 1972 and 1980. They even went close to a hat-trick, only losing in 1976 by 3–5 to Czechoslovakia on penalties.

No British team has ever reached the final – the best effort being a semi-final place by England in 1968.

The South American Championship

The South American Championship started in 1916 and was played annually until 1927. Now the final is played every four years in the year following the World Cup.

Up until 1975 the championship was decided on a points system, but since then the final has been played on a home and away basis. Uruguay and Argentina lead the way with twelve victories each. Brazil, surprisingly, have won the tournament only three times and, even more surprisingly, have not held the title since 1949.

The European, Cup Winners', and UEFA Cups

At club level the European Cup, the European Cup-Winners', and the UEFA Cup are usually thought of in that order of importance.

The European Cup is regarded as football's greatest club tournament. The first final took place in 1958 in Paris when Real Madrid beat Reims 4–3. Indeed Real Madrid were unbeatable in the first five years of the tournament, and for the first ten years the final was won by southern European clubs.

It was not until 1967 that a British club won the title. In that year Celtic beat Inter-Milan in Lisbon by 2–1 in a thrilling game with second half goals from Gemmell and Chalmers.

The following year, Manchester United beat Benfica at Wembley by 4–1 after extra time. It was an emotional occasion and a feast of football.

From 1970–76 it was the turn of central European clubs, with Ajax Amsterdam from Holland and Bayern Munich from West Germany leading the way with three victories each in the final.

From 1977–84 the pendulum swung back in Britain's favour. In 1977 Liverpool got their name on the trophy for the first time and followed up with three more wins in that period.

Nottingham Forest were 1–0 victors in 1979 and 1980 and Aston Villa in 1982. SV Hamburg were the only non-British club to record a success during this time.

The disaster of the 1985 final, when riots led to the death of forty-two people at the Heysel Stadium, Brussels, put an end to this run. English clubs were banned indefinitely from European football which seems to have suffered badly from their absence.

The European Cup is the most keenly contested club tournament in the world.

The European Cup Winners' Cup

The European Cup Winners' Cup was first held in 1960–61 when Fiorentina beat Rangers 4–1 over two legs.

There were only ten entries in the first year, possibly because European countries do not rate their national cups as highly as British countries do theirs. This is reflected in the fact that British clubs won the trophy five times out of the first ten finals – Spurs, West Ham United, Manchester City, Chelsea, and Rangers, being the successful clubs. However, the balance shifted and between 1972 and 1983 not one British name appeared on the cup.

The European Cup Winners Cup is the youngest of the three European competitions, but has proved just as popular as the other two.

The UEFA Cup

This trophy was originally known as the European Inter-City Industrial Fairs Cup, and was intended for games played between cities who held regular trade or industrial fairs.

The tournament began in 1955 and was not completed until 1958. This time span was designed to avoid clashes with regular club commitments, but it was hard to retain interest over such a long time and the competition almost died. The organizers were quick to recognize the problem

The UEFA Cup was originally intended for clubs whose city held trade fairs. It has now extended beyond this to include all European towns and cities.

and since 1961 the tournament has been annual.

For most of the sixties, continental teams ruled the competition until in 1968 Leeds United beat Ferencvaros 1–0 on aggregate to begin a period of British supremacy which brought victories also for Newcastle United, Arsenal, Leeds again, Spurs, and Liverpool.

In 1970, the name was changed to the UEFA Cup. Although considered by most to be inferior to the other two, the competition nevertheless has great prestige.

Clothing and equipment

Early days

When football was first played, players turned out in whatever they happened to be wearing at the time. The first 'uniforms' look comical to modern eyes. What looked like full-length underwear topped by a nightcap was standard wear.

Up to the late 1950s players were hindered by clumsy playing kit, especially on the lower half of the body:

Boots These were made of stiff leather, had hard toecaps, and reached above the ankle.

Socks and shinguards Socks were usually woollen which made them heavy when they became wet and muddy. Socks were padded with enormous shinguards made of strips of cane bound together by leather and horsehair. These often became itchy and hot after a time.

Shorts It is the shorts, however, which are remembered

Early players looked more suited for bedtime than a rough game of soccer!

most from those early days. People tend to forget the skill which these players had and remember only those long, baggy shorts. They must have been a handicap and one can only wonder how much quicker players might have been but for those shorts flapping around their knees.

Shirts Shirts were probably the least remarkable part of a player's kit in those days although sleeves were always long and heavyweight compared to those of today. The choice of colours was limited. Apart from one or two quarters and halves, shirts were mainly coloured, stripes or hoops, or coloured with contrasting sleeves.

The modern player

Footballers today can benefit from the advances made in textiles and materials over the last twenty years. Materials

These young Chelsea apprentices can well appreciate how many types of soccer boot are manufactured today – they have to clean most of them!

Today's soccer kit is light and cut to allow a player maximum range of movement.

such as plastic and nylon have made equipment more durable and water-resistant.

Boots Modern boots are still made primarily of leather, but are stitched with nylon thread and soled with plastic. These two artificial materials make the boot much lighter. Most boots nowadays also have interchangeable studs so that a player can still wear his favourite boots no matter what surface he is playing on.

Socks and shinguards Socks too are made of modern synthetic materials such as nylon which does not soak up the rain and mud.

Shinguards have been modified through the years probably more than any other item of a player's equipment. They now give maximum protection, are moulded to the shape of the leg, and are so light as to be hardly noticeable.

Shorts At a glance, shorts are the greatest obvious change in players' clothing. They are now modelled on the shorts athletes wear, and are cut in such a way that they do not interfere in the least with movement.

Soccer shirts are much brighter now that sponsors' names appear in the design.

Shirts The most striking feature of modern shirts are their bright colours. The synthetic fibres in these shirts can hold colours much better, so they don't fade when washed. Team shirts are also made more interesting by displaying their sponsor's name on them. Companies will pay a large amount of money for this privilege.

Many manufacturers make slight changes in their strip for the new season. The only reason they do this is to try and get you to buy a new strip before your own has worn out. Do not be fooled by them, your present kit will probably stand up to a lot more wear-and-tear.

Footballs

From the earliest days of football, games have been played with a more or less round ball. An inflated animal's bladder was first used and when that was found to burst too easily, the flexible part of its hide was used to cover it, with better results.

The design has improved over the years, but those of us whose playing days go back far enough will remember the old brown leather footballs. They absorbed water and sludge and became heavier and heavier. They stretched over the years until they were as big as beach balls and shaped like grapefruit. But worst of all they had a wicked lace which could cut you badly if you misheaded.

Nowadays balls are made of a variety of materials, but covered with a tough plastic substance which sheds water. This means that they stay light to the end of the game. It can be kicked much further and skilful players make it swerve in the air to confuse the opposition.

However, tough as it is, a ball will still last longer if it is treated with care. A few simple precautions will help your ball last even longer than usual.

- Take care when inflating the ball, especially if you are using a needle adaptor.
- Do not kick or dribble the ball on surfaces like concrete or asphalt, or near hedges with sharp thorns.
- Wash off any dirt which gathers in the case.
- Let some air out of the ball if you do not intend to use it for some time. This helps to keep it the right shape and size.

Modern soccer balls are water-resistant and so stay light until the end of the game.

Goals

The first goalposts were made of wooden planks, so the posts and crossbar were flat. Nowadays they are made of metal or fibreglass and are tubular.

There are companies who produce a range of goals suitable for every occasion from practice to full-scale games, and in all sizes. One such company in New York, USA, even makes a full-sized goal which can be assembled by one person, is so light that it can be moved anywhere around the field by two, and folds up so that it can be carried in a bag like a fishing rod!

Soccer can now be played anywhere with these five-a-side, or full-size, portable goals.

Fitness

To become a successful footballer a player must not only work on ball skills, but also on stamina, strength, speed and agility.

Stamina is the ability to keep going throughout an entire match without tiring.

Strength is required to overcome difficult conditions and tough challenges for the ball.

Speed is needed to get to the ball before the opposition, before it runs out of play, or to get past and away from the opposition.

Agility – the need for agility and elasticity is often overlooked, but the number of times a player needs to retain or regain balance during a game makes it a most important consideration.

Warm-up

Before undertaking any form of physical exercise it is most important that you warm up thoroughly beforehand. Never strain yourself during a warm-up. Everything should be done smoothly. Breathing should remain steady throughout.

Lower body

1 Stand astride the ball. Bend one knee and, keeping the other leg straight, press it down until the inside of the thigh touches the ball. Repeat with the other leg.

2 Lunge forward. The rear thigh touches the ball. Repeat with the other leg.

3 With hands on hips, bend forward until the forehead touches the ball.

4 Standing astride the ball bend both knees, and sit on the ball. At first with the heels raised and then with the feet flat on the floor.

5 Place the ball slightly in front. Crouch. From this position touch the ball with the inside of both knees or thighs.

6 Hold the ball in both hands in front of the chest, stand on tiptoe. Lift alternate knees to touch the ball. Balance.

Upper and middle body

1 Holding the ball in both hands above the head.
a Stretch as far as possible to left then to right, keeping the back straight.
b Now reach forwards as far as possible, then backwards.

2 Starting from the same position, make as large a circle as possible with the ball, moving first to the right, then to the left. When extended fully forwards, repeat the circle in the opposite direction.

3 Sit with legs straight and the ball held between the feet. Lie back until the head touches the floor. Sit up and reach forward to touch the ball with the tips of the fingers. Keep repeating until you are able to touch with the palms, wrists, etc.

4 Flat on your back with arms and legs spread and the ball held under the right arm. Swing the left leg over until it touches the ball. Repeat several times then change ball to left arm and swing right leg.

5 Hold the ball between the feet, raise it several inches above the ground then lower *slowly* to the floor.

6 Sit with legs apart, ball on the floor between the knees. Bend forward to touch the ball with the forehead.

7 Flat on your back, holding the ball between the knees. Tuck up first to the left then to the right.

8 Flat on your front. Hold the ball in both hands at arm's length and raise it, holding the position for a few seconds. Make sure your feet stay on the floor.

9 Same position. This time hold the ball in both hands behind the back. Simultaneously lift the head and shoulders off the floor and push the ball towards the feet.

1 On-off ball Ball on the floor. Stand with one foot on top of it, the other on the floor at the side of it. Jump to change feet. Count one each time you touch the top of the ball with a foot.

2 Sit-ups Ball on the floor. Lie back, hands behind the head with legs astride and straight, knees level with the ball. Sit up to touch the ball with the forehead then back to the starting position.

Strength and stamina exercise circuit

Some of the exercises in this circuit are extensions of those done in the warm-up. However, the tempo is now completely opposite to the warm-up. In the warm-up the breathing should remain slow and normal, now both breathing and heart-rate should reach a maximum.

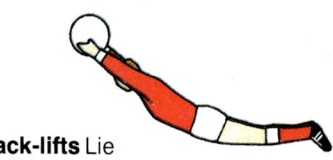

3 Back-lifts Lie full length on your front, holding the ball at arms' length. Keep the feet on the floor, raise the ball as high as possible, then lower to touch the ground.

4 Astride-squats Ball on the floor. Sit on the ball with legs astride. Jump in the air and bring the feet together above the ball, then part and bring them back to sit-astride position.

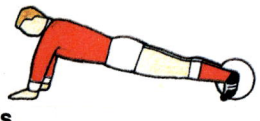

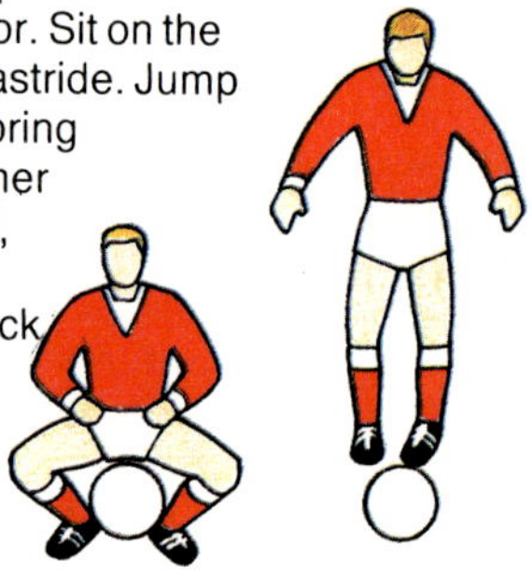

5 Squat-thrusts Front support position holding the ball between the feet. Tuck the knees up to the chest keeping the ball firmly between the feet. Return to the starting position.

6 Knee-chest Stand up holding the ball in the hands in front of the chest. Jump to touch the ball with both knees together. Count one each time the knees touch the ball.

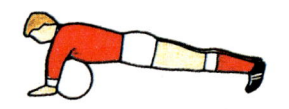

7 Press-ups Ball on the floor. In the front support position, chest above the ball. Do press-ups in the normal way, lowering until the chest touches the ball. Then push up until the arms are straight.

8 Leg-raises Flat on the back, legs straight, feet together. The ball should be held between the feet, three inches from the floor. Raise the legs a few inches and lower to the starting position.

Agility exercises

These exercises should be enjoyable and can be used for winding down at the end of your training session.

1 Sit on the ground holding the ball in both hands. Lean back and kick the ball high in the air. Get off the floor quickly and control it before it can bounce twice.

2 Hold the ball between the heels, in a standing position, with your back towards the wall. Flick it in the air behind the back, turn quickly and volley it against the wall. Control the rebound and repeat.

Endurance exercises

It is difficult to say how long players should push themselves in this type of work. If you really want to punish yourself and get fit, do these practices until your legs really ache. Rest until breathing is almost, but not quite back to normal. However, always be realistic about your general condition and don't push yourself too far.

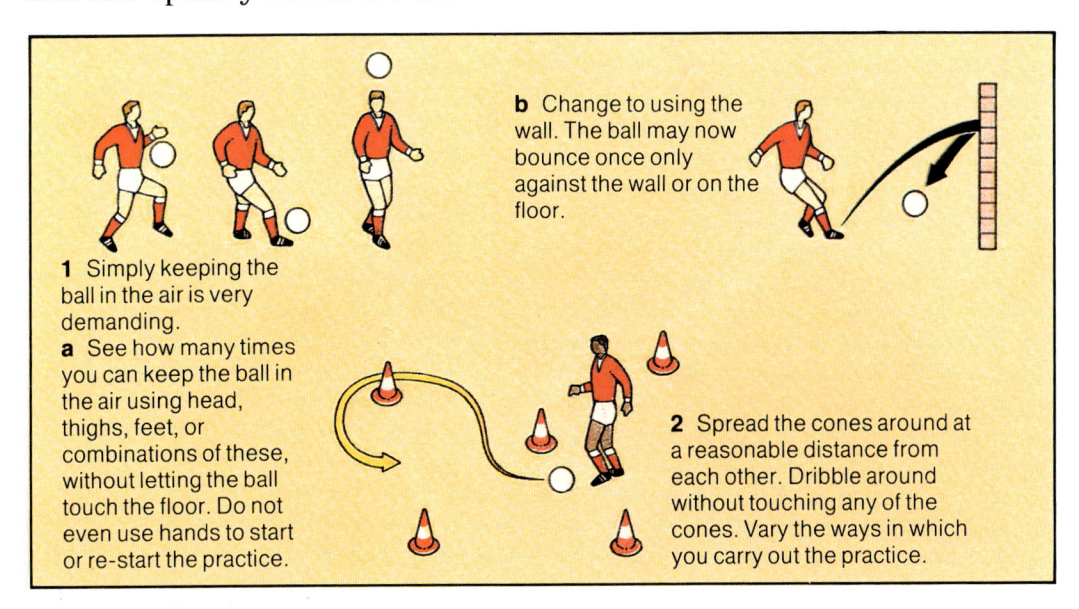

1 Simply keeping the ball in the air is very demanding.
a See how many times you can keep the ball in the air using head, thighs, feet, or combinations of these, without letting the ball touch the floor. Do not even use hands to start or re-start the practice.
b Change to using the wall. The ball may now bounce once only against the wall or on the floor.

2 Spread the cones around at a reasonable distance from each other. Dribble around without touching any of the cones. Vary the ways in which you carry out the practice.

Speed exercises

Speed off the mark rather than winning 100 m sprints is what players should really be trying to develop. Sprints in soccer are usually over little more than ten metres.

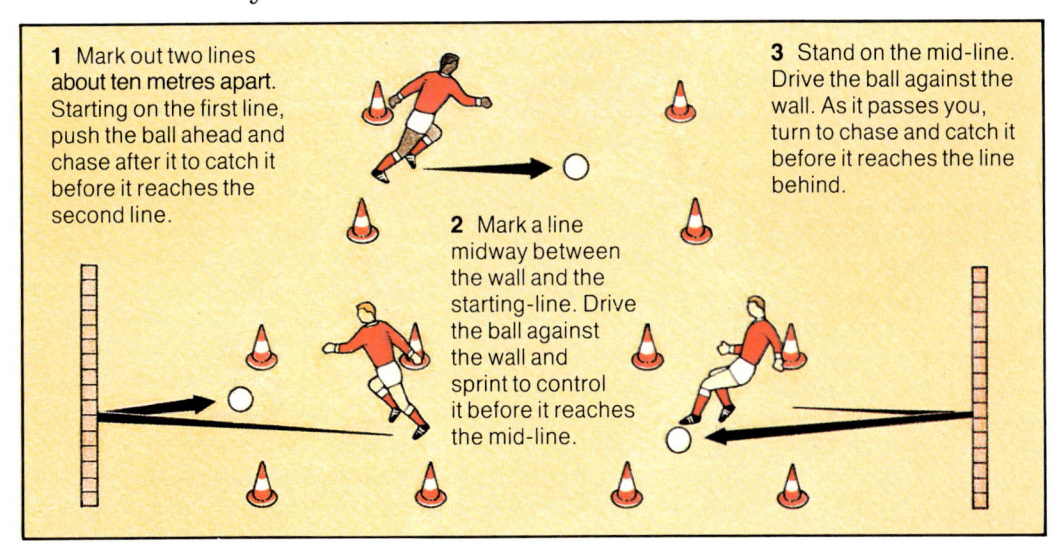

1 Mark out two lines about ten metres apart. Starting on the first line, push the ball ahead and chase after it to catch it before it reaches the second line.

2 Mark a line midway between the wall and the starting-line. Drive the ball against the wall and sprint to control it before it reaches the mid-line.

3 Stand on the mid-line. Drive the ball against the wall. As it passes you, turn to chase and catch it before it reaches the line behind.

Skills and tactics

Football places a number of demands on a player. He has to be able to stop the ball, run with it, pass the ball to another player and score goals with accurately placed shots. He also has to be able to head the ball accurately and run into useful positions around the pitch.

Passing and receiving

Passing and receiving are like Siamese twins – totally dependent on one another for survival. There is nothing more infuriating than a superbly struck pass to the feet of a receiver who allows it to bounce away out of control, or to roll under a foot and out of play. Similarly, it is a complete waste of time having players with the ability to trap the ball if their team mates persist in passing seven out of ten balls to the opposition.

Passing and receiving practice

All you need to practise your basic passing and receiving skills are a wall and a football. Strike the ball at various heights, angles and speeds to recreate different passes. Try and move into position quickly to receive and trap the ball.

Passing

Get a few of your friends and try the following exercises.
Preparation Divide yourselves into roughly two equal teams each standing in line behind a cone 20 metres apart.
Procedure The first player passes the ball as shown and then runs to the back of the opposite team and so on.
Variations Make the game two-touch – one for control and one for passing. Make the game one-touch – this takes much more skill and is much more tiring.

Checklist

Passing
- Timing: pass early to avoid being closed down.
- Weighting: firm and crisp so the ball reaches the target before it can be intercepted.
- Accuracy: decide whether the pass needs to be to feet or into space. Vary the length of pass.

Receiving
- Move quickly to the ball if it is coming straight to you.
- Use your feet to get in line if the pass is not accurate.
- Control the ball to give yourself time.
- Make as few passes as possible before shooting. Slow build-ups are less likely to create scoring chances.

Dribbling/running with the ball

There are two types of dribbling/running with the ball:
- When the player has a space in front of him to run at the opponent or space behind the opponent to run into.
- In tight situations where a player has little room to manoeuvre and has to push and weave to squeeze through. Players with the ability to dribble with the ball are an asset to any team and should be encouraged. They are match-winners if they can turn it on in the area where it counts most – near the opponent's goal.

Cones
If you are practising alone set out some cones or markers at random. Try to dribble around them in as many different ways and directions as you can.

Better still, get together with some of your friends and try the following exercise.

Preparation Mark out a small area. Each player in the practice should have a ball.

Procedure The idea is for players to move around the area with the ball at their feet, looking for space and avoiding collisions.

Variation All players in the area must try and keep possession of their own ball while at the same time looking for the chance to kick someone else's out of the area. Players who lose their own ball must leave the playing area immediately. The winner is the last player left in possession of the ball.

Checklist

- Develop the ability to move the ball with both feet.
- Develop the ability to use all the surfaces of both feet, that is, the instep, outstep, heel etc.
- Develop the ability to change direction quickly to get out of tight corners.
- In a one-against-one situation ATTACK opponents with the ball to get into the space behind.
- Make sure that when you have got past opponents, you have the speed to get away from them.
- Keep your head up to assess all the options.

Shooting

A successful coach in top-class soccer said recently in defence of a player criticized for shooting too often, that scoring goals is like winning a lottery. If you don't buy a ticket you have no chance of winning. What he meant of course is that if you shoot you may not score, but if you don't shoot you will certainly never score. So while shooting practice is no guarantee of regular goals, frequent practice at hitting the target, getting into the right area and making the right angles must all increase the chances of success.

Shooting practice

Mark out a number of bricks at various heights on a wall with chalk and try to hit each one in turn. For low shots keep your head down and body well over the ball, for the high shots lean back more as you kick the ball.

One-touch shooting drill

Preparation Mark out an area as shown in the picture below. There should be no goalkeeper at this stage. One ball is needed.

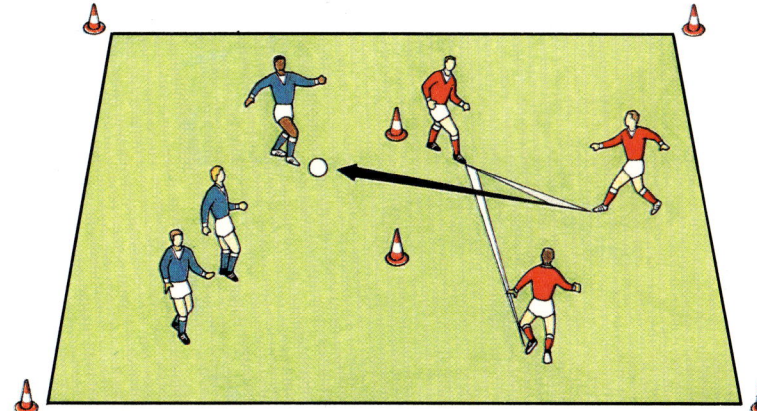

Procedure The aim of the drill is for each player to touch the ball once with the third player making a first-time shot at goal. When the ball has crossed the line dividing the groups, the other group tries to do the same thing without stopping the action. In this way the drill becomes continuous.

If you are unable to get enough players you can do the same drill but hit the final shot against a wall.

Variation 1. Number the players 1, 2 & 3. They must now make the final shot at goal in turn. This prevents the same player from hogging all the shots.

2. Bring in a goalkeeper and widen the goals. The outside players will now have to make more adjustments because they will position themselves for a ball coming straight through, but if the goalkeeper makes a save, they will have to re-adjust for a throw out.

Checklist

- Hit the target. Power is no good if the shot is wide of the goal.
- Keep your eye on the ball as you strike it and keep your head down for a fraction after.
- Don't be afraid to shoot. Very often, passing the ball means passing the responsibility.
- Make sure someone follows the shot in, goalkeepers often only parry a shot.

Defending

Team defence

It is important to remember that as soon as the other team has the ball, every player in your team is a defender with a duty to win the ball back as quickly as possible. The nearer to the opponents' goal the ball is won the sooner a strike can be made. The more often the ball is won early, the less tiring the game becomes. This is particularly true at our level where players are less fit than the professionals.

Pressure must be put on the player with the ball immediately. Then, as soon as possible, put pressure on the players nearest to the ball. This means that opponents are denied the chance to play themselves easily out of trouble. They are forced instead to attempt hopeful, more risky, long passes.

In all defensive situations try to have one player more than your opponents. This provides cover if one defender is beaten.

Winning the ball contest

Preparation You will need at least two other players and a football for this exercise. Line up in a pair, or pairs, approximately 20 metres from your coach.

Procedure Play a ball gently towards the first pair. When the ball has travelled a few yards shout "Go!"
The players then come forward off the line, compete to win the ball, and give a controlled pass back to the coach.

Variation 1. Vary the starting position of the players. Have them facing away from you, lying down etc.
2. Change partners frequently so that players who are regularly beaten don't lose interest.

Checklist

- Aim to be first to the ball.
- If not, prevent your opponent from turning.
- Stay on your feet. Only slide-tackle as a last resort to stop a cross or a shot.
- Stay close so that your opponent has to keep his eyes on the ball.
- Try to make your opponent pass sideways or backwards.
- Give information to other defenders as the opposition attacks.

Heading

Heading is a skill unique to football. No other sport uses the head to propel the ball. Many young players are afraid of heading a high ball. This fear can be overcome by regular practice in training sessions. It is best to start with the basics and build up to more difficult exercises.

Procedure

Stand about five metres back from a wall and throw the ball against it. As it rebounds run forward and head it back against the wall. Vary the height and power of your throws, but always try to head the ball straight back against the wall.

Head tennis

Preparation Divide the players into two equal teams. Mark out a court of appropriate size. Divide the court in half as shown on page 57 with a 'no-go' area in the middle.

Procedure The game is similar to tennis. Points are scored when the ball bounces twice in an opponents' half or when an opponent returns the ball out of court. The main difference is that feet and head are used instead of racquets. The ball may be kept in the air any number of times with the head or foot but it must be headed into the opponent's half.

Variations This game can be played with two players heading the ball over the crossbar to each other. You should aim to keep the ball in the air as long as possible rather than trying to beat your opponent.

Checklist

- Heading normally demands power – this comes from the whole body, not just from waggling the head at the ball. a) Use the legs to jump. b) Flex the trunk. c) Brace the neck and use the forehead.
- Remember the sequence: a) Run to get into position. b) Take off on one foot. c) Meet the ball at its highest point, move through it. d) Make firm contact.
- Head downwards for goal, upwards for clearance.
- The player who gets off the ground first is usually favourite to win the ball.

Goalkeeping

A goalkeeper needs special qualities, different from his colleagues'. Goalkeepers need strength and courage, sharp reflexes and agility and good eyesight and judgement. It is also an advantage if you are tall, but this can be made up for by developing your 'spring' or ability to leap high.

It would be impossible to cover all the technical elements in such a short space, but the following exercises will develop the necessary skills.

Agility

1. The server tosses the ball high for the goalkeeper to run, jump and catch at its highest point.

2. The service is identical, but this time the goalkeeper does a forward roll towards the server before jumping to catch the ball in the same way.

3. The service is identical. This time the goalkeeper faces away from the server and does a forward roll away from the server before jumping with a turn to catch the ball.

Notes
1. The goalkeeper must always try to move through the ball, not upwards and underneath it.
2. The goalkeeper has the leading knee high for protection, not as a weapon.

Endurance
1. Place three or four balls a few yards away from goal. Each is driven at intervals for the goalkeeper to stop in any way possible. The rest period comes whilst the balls are replaced.

2. The goalkeeper stands on the edge of the goal area facing the server who lobs the ball over the goalkeeper's head. The goalkeeper runs backwards to try to stop the ball going into the goal.

Speed
1. The goalkeeper stands at the corner of the goal. The server rolls or lobs the ball to the far corner of the goal. The goalkeeper must try to stop it from crossing the goal line.

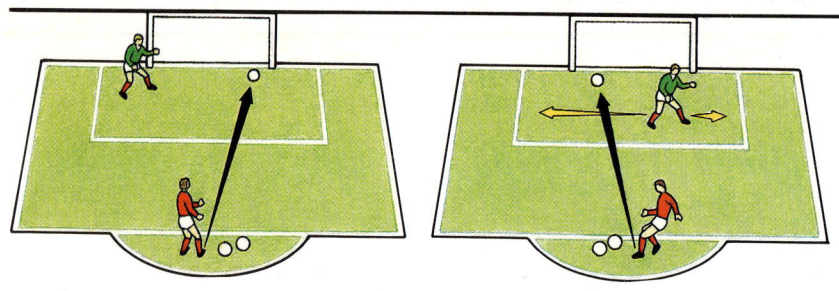

2. The goalkeeper moves a few paces to either side in turn. The server tries to fool the goalkeeper by hitting a shot to the opposite side to the one in which the goalkeeper is moving. The goalkeeper must quickly adjust to save.

Notes
1. This tests speed of movement sideways across the goal and quick adjustment of position.
2. In exercise 1 try the goalkeeper in different starting positions e.g. kneeling, sitting, lying down.

Reflexes
1. The goalkeeper faces the server who drives the ball against a wall. The goalkeeper must turn to stop the ball before it can go past.

2. The goalkeeper faces the wall. The server throws the ball at various heights against the wall and the keeper must catch and hold it each time.
3. Goalkeeper and server again, or two goalkeepers. The players face each other: one with the ball, the other with legs apart. The player with the ball plays it through the goalkeeper's legs. The goalkeeper turns and pounces on the ball before it can escape. Great agility is needed as the goalkeeper must turn and take off all in one movement.

Remarkable feats

Longest match
The longest match was played in the Copa Libertadores in Santos, Brazil, on 2–3 August, 1962, when Santos drew 3–3 with Penarol FC of Montevideo, Uruguay. The game lasted 3½ hours (with interruptions) from 9.30 pm to 1 am.

Longest unbeaten streak
Nottingham Forest were unbeaten in 42 consecutive Division one matches from 20 November 1977 to 9 December 1978. In Scottish football, Glasgow Celtic were unbeaten in 62 matches (49 won, 13 drawn), from 13 November 1915 to 21 April 1917.

Goal scoring

Teams
The highest score recorded in a first-class match is 36 goals. This happened in the Scottish Cup match between Arbroath and Bon Accord on 5 September 1885, when Arbroath won 36–0 on their home ground. Many more would have been scored if it hadn't been for the lack of nets and so the loss of time retrieving the ball.
The highest margin recorded in an international match is 17. At the England v Australia match at Sydney on 30 June 1951, England won 17–0. This match is not listed by England as a full international. The highest in the British Isles was when England beat Ireland 13–0 at Belfast on 18 February 1882.

Career
The most goals scored in a career is 1,216 by Edson Arantes do Nascimento (b. Bauru, Brazil, 23 October, 1940), known as Pele, the Brazilian inside left, from 7 September 1956 to 2 October 1974 in 1,254 games. His best year was 1959 with 126 goals and the milesimo (1000th) came in a penalty for his club Santos in the Maracana Stadium, Rio de Janeiro on 19 November 1969 when playing his 909th first-class match. He later played for New York Cosmos and on his retirement on 1 October 1977 his total had reached 1,281 goals, in 1,363 games.

Fastest goals

The fastest goal was scored in 6 seconds by Albert Mundy (Aldershot) in a Division Four match v. Hartlepool United at Victoria Ground, Hartlepool, Cleveland on 25 October 1958. This record is also held by Barrie Jones of Notts County, 1962; Keith Smith of Crystal Palace, 1964; Tommy Langley of QPR, 1980.

The fastest confirmed hat-trick is in 2½ minutes by Ephraim 'Jock' Dodds for Blackpool v Tranmere Rovers on 28 February 1943.

Fastest own goal

Torquay United's Pat Kruse equalled the fastest goal on record when he headed the ball into his own net only six seconds after kick-off against Cambridge United on 3 January 1977.

Players

The greatest number of appearances for a national team is 145 by Hector Chumpitaz (Peru) from 1963 to 1981. This includes all matches played by the national team.

Bobby Moore, of West Ham United and Fulham set up a new record of full international appearances by a British footballer by playing in his 108th game for England v Italy on 14 November 1973 at Wembley. His first appearance was against Peru on 20 May 1962 and he retired from professional football on 14 May 1977 on his 1000th appearance in all matches.

Heaviest goalkeeper

The biggest goalkeeper in representative football was the England international Willie J. 'Fatty' Foulke (1874–1916), who stood 1.90m and weighed 141 kg. His last games were for Bradford City, by which time he was 165 kg. He once stopped a game by snapping the cross bar.

Attendances

The greatest recorded crowd at any football match was 205,000 (199,854 paid) for the Brazil v Uruguay World Cup match in the Maracana Municipal Stadium, Rio de Janeiro, Brazil on 16 July 1950.

Ball control

Mikael Palmqvist (20) juggled a soccer ball for ten hours non-stop at Traffens in Sweden on 8 May, 1980. He did 80,357 repetitions with feet, legs and head without the ball ever touching the ground.

Glossary

Aggregate The final score in a match when the results of the home and away games have been added together.
Agility The ability to react quickly and nimbly.
Centre or crossed ball A ball played from the edge of the pitch into the goalmouth.
Dribbling Running with the ball under close control at your feet.
Drills A set of repeated exercises.
Marking Remaining close to an opponent to prevent them from becoming involved in the game.
Outfield players All the players except the goalkeeper.
Shinguards Strips of padded plastic placed inside the socks to protect the lower leg.
Sponsorship Money contributed to a club by a company. In return the company's name will appear on the players' shirts and inside the ground.
Terraces The area in a football ground where the spectators stand to watch the match.
Transfer When a player moves from one club to another, usually for a sum of money.
Trapping the ball Bringing the ball under control with the feet or legs.

Books to read

Football by Gerhard Bauer (EP Publishing Ltd., 1979)
Football, Techniques and Tactics by Richard Widdows (Hamlyn, 1984)
Laws of Association Football by The Football Association (1986)
Successful Soccer by Bobby Brown (Charles Letts, 1980)
The Observer's Book of Soccer by Albert Sewell (Frederick Warne, 1984)
Soccer Cards by John Riley (1980)
Soccer Laws Illustrated by Stanley Lover (Pelham Books)

Useful addresses

Football Association
16 Lancaster Gate
London
W2 3LW

Scottish Football League
188 West Regent Street
Glasgow
Strathclyde
G2 4RY

Referees Association
126 Whitehorse Common Road
Sutton Coldfield
Birmingham

Index

Argentina 25, 39
Asia 23
Attack 16, 21, 25, 54
Australia 13
Austria 8

Balls 4, 6, 16, 17, 21, 22, 23, 24, 48–9, 53, 55, 56, 57, 59, 60
Barcelona 28–9
Bayern Munich 29–30
Belgium 12, 25, 40
Brazil 25, 30, 39
Britain 4, 5, 7, 8, 10, 11, 12, 13, 17, 25, 33, 40

Celtic 27–9, 35
Championships 38–42
China 4
Clubs 6, 11, 12, 15, 17, 18, 22, 27, 28, 29, 31, 32, 34, 40
  European 11, 12
  professional 22
Coaches 15, 16, 17, 20, 21, 54, 56
Crowds 9, 29, 31, 35, 37
Czechoslovakia 8, 39

Defence 16, 21, 25, 56, 57
Denmark 25
Dribbling 53, 54

Emerging nations 13–14
Equipment 43–48
Europe 8, 13, 23, 26, 29, 39, 40
Exercises 48, 49, 50, 51, 56, 57, 60

Federation of Indoor Football in the USA (FIFUSA) 23
Federation of International Football Associations (FIFA) 8
Fitness 48, 51
Flamengo 30
Football Association 6, 21
Football League 7, 12

Goalkeepers 15, 16, 17, 18, 19, 20, 23, 24, 25, 55, 58, 59, 60
Goals 4, 6, 16, 19, 21, 24, 29, 30, 47, 54, 55, 58, 59, 60
Goram, Andy 15–20

Heading 57, 58
History 5, 12, 26, 27
Holland 12, 25
Hooliganism 32, 40
Hungary 8

Italy 12, 25, 29, 40

Japan 4
Juventus 29

Liverpool 26–7, 30, 40, 42

Managers 16, 26–7, 28
Matches 7, 17, 20, 21
  eleven-a-side 21, 22
  five-a-side 22, 23
  four v four 21–2
  indoor 23, 24
  informal 21
  international 7, 8
  league 16, 29, 30
  professional 14
  six-a-side 24
  small-sided 22, 23
  televised 9
Mexico 15
Major Indoor Soccer League (MISL) 24

North American Soccer League 14

Passing 24, 52, 53, 55, 56
Pitches 23, 24, 31
  artificial 11–12, 15, 18, 47
Players 5, 12, 14, 15, 16, 17, 21, 25, 26, 27, 28, 29, 32, 38, 43, 48, 52, 55, 56, 57, 58
  foreign 12, 13

  outfield 16, 18, 19, 21, 22
  professional 20, 21, 22
  reserves 12
  women 10
  young 11–12, 14, 18, 21, 22, 57
Portugal 13, 40
Practice 52, 53, 54, 55, 56, 57, 58, 59

Receiving 52, 53
Rules 4, 6, 23, 24

Scotland 15, 25
Scottish Football Association 7, 17
Skills 15, 16, 22, 26, 48, 52, 57, 58
Spain 12, 25, 28, 40
Sponsorship 10–11, 38
South America 13, 23, 39
Stadiums 12, 18, 28, 31, 32, 33, 36
  Bernabeu 37
  Ibrox 35–6
  Maracana 30, 37
  Old Trafford 34–5
  stands 31, 32, 33, 34, 36
  terraces 31
  Wembley 33, 34
Switzerland 12–13

Tackling 22
Teams 17, 21, 24, 25, 26, 36, 53, 56
Training 12, 15, 18, 19, 22
Transfers 12

United States Minisoccer Federation (USMF) 23
United States Soccer Federation (USSF) 14
USA 9, 10, 11, 14, 23, 24, 47
USSR 25

Wales 25
Warm-up 16, 48
West Germany 12, 25, 29, 30, 39
Women's Football Association 10
World Cup Finals 4, 15